She Plays Sports

# She Plays Softball

By Trudy Becker

level 2 little blue readers

**www.littlebluehousebooks.com**



Little Blue House is distributed by North Star Editions:
sales@northstareditions.com | 888-417-0195

Produced for Little Blue House by Red Line Editorial.

Photographs ©: Shutterstock Images, cover, 9 (top) , 9 (bottom), 10–11, 19 (top), 23 (top), 24 (top right), 24 (bottom left); iStockphoto, 4, 7, 12, 15, 19 (bottom), 21, 23 (bottom), 24 (top left); Pexels, 16, 24 (bottom right)

**Library of Congress Control Number: 2022910480**

**ISBN**
978-1-64619-711-8 (hardcover)
978-1-64619-743-9 (paperback)
978-1-64619-803-0 (ebook pdf)
978-1-64619-775-0 (hosted ebook)

Printed in the United States of America
Mankato, MN
012023

## About the Author

Trudy Becker lives in Minneapolis, Minnesota. She likes exploring new places and loves anything involving books.

# Table of Contents

# Getting Ready

I play softball.

I love game days.

I get ready to play.

I find my uniform.
I wear pants and
long socks.
I wear a jersey too.

jersey

I put on my cap.
I put on my cleats too.
They help me run on
the dirt.

cap

cleats

I need my softball bat to
hit the ball.
I also grab my glove.

softball bat
glove

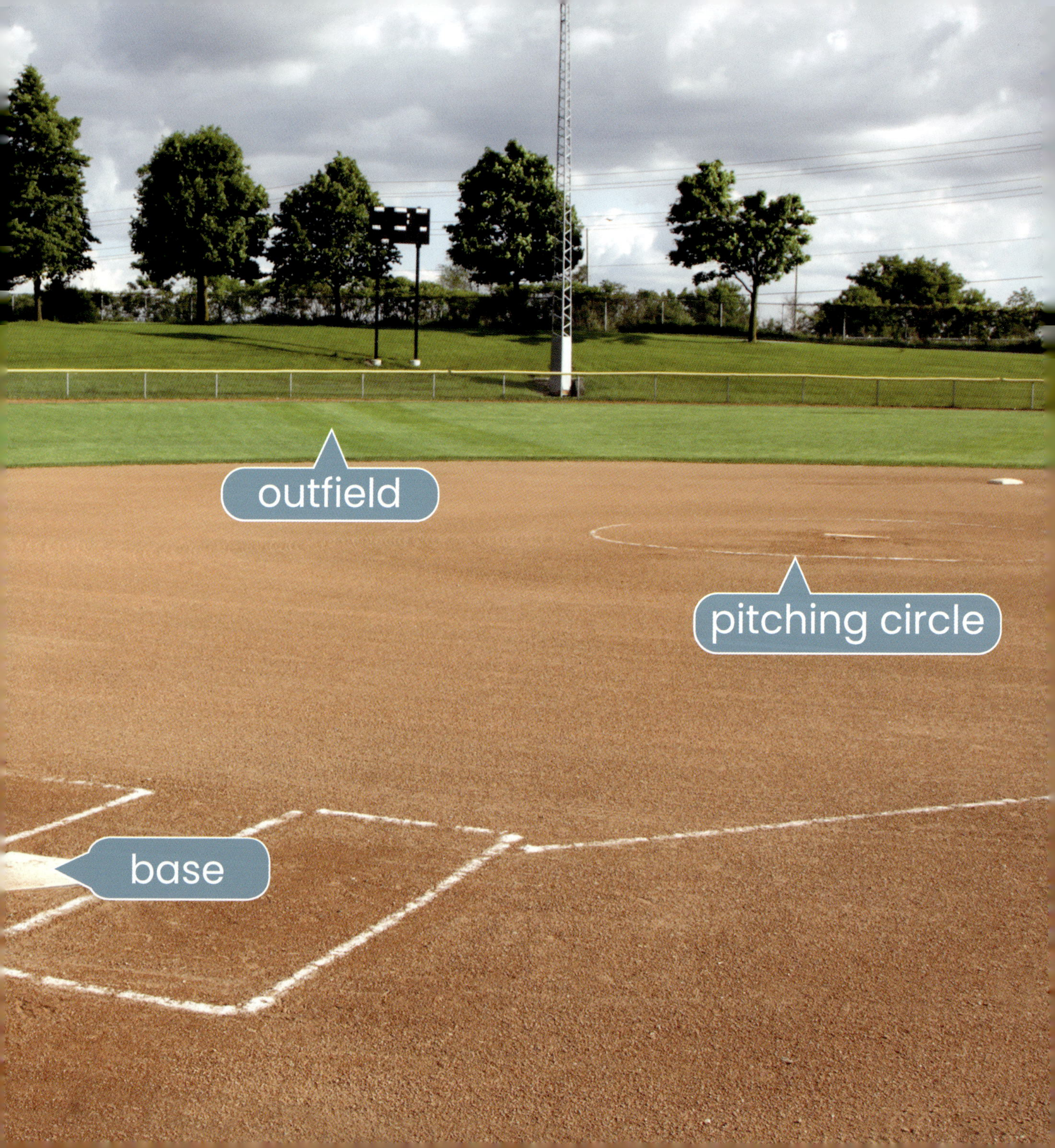
outfield
pitching circle
base

# On the Field

Games happen at the softball field.

There are bases in the dirt.

In the middle is the pitching circle.

There is a green outfield too.

Before each game starts,
I find my position.
Sometimes I play in
the outfield.
I punch my glove to
get ready.

HOME PITCH COUNT GUEST
OUT
TOTAL

pitcher

# In the Game

I focus when the game starts. Sometimes I am the pitcher. I throw the ball hard over the plate.

When a batter hits
the ball my way, I run
toward it.
I catch the ball in
my glove.
The batter is out!

batter

Sometimes it is my turn to bat.

I swing at the pitch.

I drop the bat and run toward first base.

The ball flies over
the fence.
I hit a home run!
The crowd cheers, and I
run around the bases.
I love softball.

# Glossary

base

glove

cleats

pitcher

# Index